At the Border of Wilshire *&* Nobody

At the Border of Wilshire & Nobody

POEMS

Marci Vogel

HOWLING BIRD PRESS

2015

MINNEAPOLIS

AT THE BORDER OF WILSHIRE & NOBODY
Poems
Copyright © 2015 Marci Vogel
Winner of the 2015 Howling Bird Press Poetry Prize

ISBN: 978-0-9961952–0–1

•

HOWLING BIRD PRESS
MFA in Creative Writing
Augsburg College
2211 Riverside Avenue
Minneapolis, Minnesota 55454
www.augsburg.edu/mfa

•

Book design: Amanda Symes, Ashley Cardona, Kevin Matuseski, John Gaterud
Text: Adobe Garamond Pro
Poem titles: Helvetica Neue

Cover & author photographs copyright © 2015 Peter Figen
www.peterfigen.com
Cover design: Kristin Higginbotham

Printed at BookMobile, Minneapolis
First printing

For my kindred—through blood, marriage, friendship & beyond—love beyond measure.

Contents

I

II

I

Panorama Highway

1.

We take it north, past
Mulholland Bridge, spanning cars, clouds, past
the expanse of auto parts places and trophy shops, far from the ocean,
into a land of flat surrounded by mountains. Arriving to California by train, my mother
marvels at how the earth changes its height. In winter, through the picture window of my
childhood home, snow changes it again. Is there a question you are holding? Ask it now.

2.

What do we do when we're supposed
to be driving? Listen to jazz, I mean listen with our whole
bodies. Write poems in our heads, or even on paper. I watched a woman read once,
not a Blackberry, but a real book. She opened it, set the spine right on her steering wheel.
The usual: apply lipstick; examine teeth, ears, tongue. Make love. I once tried meditation
for busy people, except for the part where you shut your eyes. All the way down the 405,
may we be protected from inner and outer harm; may we be happy; may we be well.

3.

The 405 out to the Valley
is bumpy, filled with potholes
the county is too broke to repair. Was it Rome
that invented roads, their chariots traveling a network of paving? We take this one
beyond the living, to the edge of where we bury our dead with a view of the freeway.
They say people were captured in ash before breakfast. The traffic thins at Pyramid
Lake. I look out to see steps carved into the side of the mountain, the rising and falling.

4.

If you could hold
one word in the palm of your hand,
which? Cloud, from which the whole
story springs: rain, blood, seventy-five percent of our bodies. How generous the long
grass moves so that we might see the wind when traveling with the windows rolled shut.

5.

The sky, a field
of white. Expand your gaze
to see a red truck pass, crops readying
their harvest, birds spiraling in a cone of play.

6.

Your mind
the sky, wide
over Highway 5, each thought
a passing truck, a power structure, the aqueduct
snaking water to the south, where you will splash your face until you wake up.

7.

On the way from the parking lot,
a young man with a clipboard asks
Would you like to help save the world? and I want
to, only I've left the reusable bags in the trunk, and the ice
cream is melting, and I'm trying to stay in the moment. I unload the cart, drive up
to the woman in the booth, smile, hand her a pink ticket. The gate opens, the car merges.

8.

Some days, we fly
across the first interchange designed
by a woman, long curves, *a work of art as a pattern
on the map, as a monument against the sky, and as a kinetic experience as you sweep
through it*, wrote someone important. She said it was built to keep traffic moving at high
speeds, *so you don't have to slam on the brakes.* Today, we are stopped in the curve's
center. Look through the passenger window: buildings, houses, a temple in the mountain.

O steepled world,

Let there be wild licorice firecrackering yellow,
greenheartful middle sheltering the tiniest sparrows,
dandelion stars seeding the air. This morning I saw

a man with fir trees
inked on the flesh of each calf, two trees walking
the parched earth, & on the hill's top, a tai chi

master arcing slow blessings over us—young
woman climbing in a faded apron, infant
fastened to chest, gray-bearded man who used to be

fast. O city that waters desert, dry these cries,
wash my crumbs to the sea, & open my
lips that my words may declare your glory.

My Father, on the Small Screen

My father was an extra
in the *Ten Commandments*,
where he played soldier
to pharaoh, not a slave,
but not a free man either. He
was not one of the throng led
to Canaan's land by Charlton
Heston over the floor of the ocean,
on the way to honeyed manna, past
the surprised fish. Muscled,
tanned with Santa Monica sun,
my father ate Roman Meal bread
for breakfast and was in too good
a shape to serve anyone
but the king. When Moses
approached that burning
bush, lifted high the tablets,
my father was back in his own
Egypt, trespassing against
at least one commandment: *Thou
shall not kill*. He was clever, my
father, found a loophole, slipped
it around his neck. Every Passover,
my brother and I were permitted
to stay up too late on a school night
to witness my father's appearance
on TV, where he cast his image
upon the Technicolor desert. All these years
later, I still watch, searching for a glimpse
of his beautiful form.

A Retrospective of Birds

Iridescence
Pre-Millennium 3, AD
Glass bowl with mosaic inlay
Tesserae of nectar, rapid movement, twelve-hundred heartbeats per second

Merely by shifting position, a muted-looking bird will suddenly become fiery red or vivid green. However, not all hummingbird colors are due to the prism feather structure. Brilliance results from refraction and pigmentation, the way light from another's face bends dullness to beauty. During courtship displays, the wings of the smallest birds reach one hundred beats per second. Only hours away from starving to death, hummingbirds store just enough energy to survive overnight, every morning a miraculous fluttering in the hand.

Nest
2005
5,932 square-foot lot
Mixed media: wood, stucco, soil, water

Birds of paradise congregate in an earthly aerie, established roots, orange crowns open. Toward the center of the composition, tiny house sparrows nestle in a butterfly bush by the kitchen window. Behind the glass, a woman studies new flight as she washes wedding dishes on the verge of shatter.

In the upper left, note the human neighbor, passing lemons over the fence.

Valiant

Strip the fruit of passion's tango
                                  through a stop-gapped smile

steeped with sugar and lemon,
                                  tongue-glazed enamel. *Let's*

get to gettin', missy. Palms open, we wanted
                                  for nothing, before a dancing torso

stepped us into a room where we saw
                                  that we were not Miss America

Pie, but Cat Woman, scratching lights off in a windy
                                  cavern, taunts sharp at the X-acto

nave of the throat. After school, we climbed into that faded pink
                                  car, *Sturm und Drang* all the way home. Steep

corners on the cliffs of the back seat. No belts. The door opened once,
                                  and one of us slid right out.

The Law of Hospitality Breaks Our Foundation

We bought a book once:
Reasons Not to Travel: strange
food, crazy people,
easy to get lost, better to stay
home—which we did, grateful
not to be tourists or even more heroic
adventurers, Keats sailing the Spanish
Steps or Odysseus fighting on foreign fields, far
from circumspect wife, their rooted bed,
unbearded son, loyal dog. One domestic
evening, an exile rang our bell: if we were not venturing
out, he would come in, make himself
at home in your leather chair, take
the seat opposite
me at the kitchen table, sleep
on your side of our bed.

Oh, he
stayed longer than a polite three
days, never removing his black
gloves, long coat, villain's hat. No flash
photography permitted. How long he
would stay abroad in your psyche, I couldn't
foresee, only thought often of Penelope
weaving her husband's return on an unfriendly
sea, Athena's owl wisdom swooping
to rescue where wile failed, wondered if we too
had a patron goddess who might end
the journey of our unkind visitor, and after
he left, how we would head out, just as the old warrior
stepped ashore, nothing too far—
maybe Spain, maybe Greece, maybe Rome
after the fall.

Missing Our Red Chow, I Consider

how she wasn't really red, but
more persimmon, ripened
after the leaves have fallen,
orange balls like paper lanterns,
lion hearted, with fur that matched
the wood floors of our old house, striated layers
of grained oak, upon which she ruled
over us and the forlorn gray
cat who now paces the empty
porch, next to the birds
of paradise, clamoring
with their mandarin beaks. We named her
Tang, after the tangerine elixir
of astronauts somersaulting
gravity's Earth, and as a bow
to her ancient homeland,
where she once protected
poets and painters. I take up
my words, you your colors.
In the far corner
of the realm, Tang takes her
final rest under a young
maple, five months planted,
leaves unfurled to a dynasty
of orange.

The Depression Scales

Are they found
sheening fish? Or
are they blackness
the mountain

ascends? Maybe
submerged weights,
chaining one
to ten. From what drop

does your heart
sheer? Into what range
do your hopes
fall? How to measure

what is not? If I press
your body here,
will my finger
leave a mark?

In Surprise, Arizona

An eye doctor, a heart center
on every corner, like churches or beauty
salons Some Other Places, so many

eyes failing, hearts exhausted
by no practice, years beating
oxygen choked pollution.

The eye is made to see things,
types the mystic poet. What about
clouded corneas, detached

retinas, cones unresponsive
to light? And the heart: does it
share the soul's joy, or are they

only silvered words inscribed
around my neck? My friend
took her dying mother not to the desert

but to the sea, where they treated
her so well, she lived longer
than anyone expected. I've heard

the eye stops viewing things no longer
important to see, that a heart can

beat even after we are dead.

Domestic Still Life

We heard only
the shudder of a jet
approaching louder,
but it could have been
the end of the world,
and it wouldn't have
mattered. I was in
the kitchen, washing
dishes, soaring through
the window, the light
that brilliance right
before the mist takes
over, speakers sounding
a kind of blue almost
remembered. You were
here but not, close
enough where I could
turn my head to see
you somewhere
else. No dog clattered
worn tags on the linoleum
floor, a swell of
piano and engine
converging at
the exact moment
where my hands slipped
under filmy water, the crash
of glass on enamel
so much quieter
than I ever imagined.

We Find Ourselves Immersed

in a billion droplets
condensed at the summit
of Haleakala, where we have

long wanted to swim together,
a sure saturation, vision misted,
treading crystallized vapor. A silver
band of a thousand fish schools us

in coral depths as we snorkel
above green sea turtles, their paddles
sweeping ancient carapaces, back
and forth like windshield wipers

across the window of the rented
car that delivers us into air,
where we fly over dolphins
twirling in blue waters, an ocean of salt

rimming the shore of Los Angeles.
Back in the desert, one of us opens
Pandora's box, and a tropical storm
surges out: *A stick, a stone, it's the end*

of the road. It's the rest of a stump, it's
a little alone. I lace up my fins, backstroke
through mud, the plan of our house, your body
in bed. On a wet sidewalk, a jacaranda

seedpod glistens black, a spot on
a giraffe, liquid eye blinking back
tender lashes. Does he apprehend
the recent baptism, the unusual lack

of drought the first time we set up
our tent without
the man who showed us how
to be married well (enclosing all,

even the shape of loss)? Silent,
he blows glass kisses: *Tell
my wife I love her still.*
Evaporated water

leaves a mark
around the rising circle
of grief, eddying in laps,
over cheek, down floor,

back to the new widow,
adrift and fathoming
on a straight-backed chair
if she begins tears—

What To Do About Loss

You can close it up—
zip, zip, zip
key in the lock.

You can drink it down,
fill the cup,
tilt back the chin.

You can break the shine—
smash, smash, smash
against the wall.

What is it this life
wants us to
hold? Each other,

close as our own breath
through the body—
in out in.

In Transit

Between departure &
       arrival, I stumbled

upon an abandoned terminal,
       sat in a retired Corbusier chair,
pretended to be traveling well

while birds raced planes outside
       the window, an entire flock, birds
             so small, they could have been moths

in a low-clouded sky mixed with
       metal & steel & a cemented expanse
of take-off, each its own particular shade of gray

startled by glowing vests tending to jets as if
       they were horses, feeding, watering, removing
stays from underneath stationary wheels. I remained

immobile, watched distant trees that seemed
       to reel forward as a yellow train
rhythmed by & cars motored in the opposite

             direction. A man begged my pardon,
       inquired if I was headed to Detroit. Next,
a flight attendant in a blue suit: *If you're*

traveling this century, the plane is boarding
       soon. I checked my watch, repacked ancient wax
wings. What is this gate beyond rivers where

       fellow travelers lift each other
into voyages? See her, waving goodbye.

The Moon Over Mars

The moon's not so bad, but I refuse Mars
all his heated redness, compacted
soil, hard-life planet, mean
with war. Of the moon, there are places enough
that seem familiar, like those photographs
in *World Book* of dust & craters,
somewhere between desolation and
surrender: Mojave, Haleakala, vacated acres
some would claim as their own.

                  I could float
tethered to spacecraft, gaze back
from the pull of her orbit, except I would long

too much for home, every 24-hour rotation, the slow
revolution around the sun; too sad to watch
all the blue seeping out. Maybe rivers flow
through underground Martian channels, ancient ice locked
in lunar craters, but the only waters
I desire are Earth's, those seas, cumulus, salt, fresh
in our skin, our bodies, our breath, hot moist
on a window where we write
we were here, we didn't

love you enough, we're sorry
we left.

The Situation Room Is Gutted Down to Brick & Bare Floor

one day we will gather in what used to be the main square

of our now abandoned village, particles of radioactive lodged

in heart, lung diaphragm moving the breath of

dinosaurs through us human ancestors there is no new

air, only what has already been taken in & exhaled

over millennia we will gather in the exclusion zone of

our former home no longer abandoned there will be no

situation room no bird unable to sustain its lift, no

human courier & we will gather around an empty

square & they will transmit a record into the atmosphere

into forever, squaring forever, the way mirror squares mirror

Liquid Takes the Shape of Its Container

What I was after was never-
ending line, long waves under cirrus sky, fish swimming over a margin of error, too narrow, no retainer. I wanted leaped building &

lifted twirl, the escape artist's tricks, vast orbit of skirt. I wanted an open

carriage, crown aligned with tiara, wing on scapula, triangles unhinged, words spilling out. I wanted

silk parachute, breath a straight shot. I wanted a driver, fully veiled & unarrested
humming at the sign where pedestrians cross. She is named after

one of those M states, Missouri or Montana, one of those horizontal places with Cartesian plains
& iconic rivers. State of mind, state of grace, state of flux, ever-changing third state of matter. Molecules in suspension, viscous,

slender needle floating on surface tension. Liquid supercooled toward the glass transition. *I wish I had not been*

so reserved, said Joseph Cornell on the day of his death. She lifts her

foot off the brake, skims by black-eyed Susans planted in the meridian, all their yellow pulled into ponytails. I wanted to sponsor wild
horses. Look closely: dark centers, not black. When she grows up, she wants

to be the big bad wolf, blowing houses down without getting caught. *Do not turn to ghosts &*
do not inquire of familiar spirits. Of your harvest, leave a portion ungleaned. Ask not the young men racing full force

up the stairs, weights on chests as if they were in combat & maybe they are. I wanted running towards each other, as if we were
not strangers

on a morning sidewalk, as if we were slow-motion lovers. I trail a couple with a Leica camera. He wears the lens
around his neck. She hasn't taken a picture since 1996, doesn't know how to download anything but film. They are working on a

landscape view, putting in roses, wanting us
to turn the book in our hands. Did you know my specified spirit

is listed on your checkout basket? Did you want
the woman on the prow of my ship to place carved lips to salted brow? I promise she will

stitch hemispheres whole. She wants to be a magpie gathering shine, brimming eyes. Her border blurs

magnolia blossoms, perfect votives across the leaves of a dark table. She passes a young man, tall as he will ever
grow. He wears a plaid shirt, passes his hand over indigenous grasses. Back in port, she'll say I wanted planets

of space, did not want to shuttle along. I wanted what the men had, the stars, the moon, the sun
in the center of the universe. It cost

Galileo his life. Remember that time you fell out
your side of the bed as if you were leaping, as if you were drowning & shouted yes, the boat was sinking & called me to jump, too?

Lines Composed Over No Cup of Tea at the Border of Wilshire & Nobody

No coins for a cup,
neither does anyone
else have. I take
the only empty seat

in a long row of black
chairs, spend months—
years—skimming
stones across

the river by Hope's
house.
        Days crossed
on an expired

calendar, hammer
and chisel clearly
discernible in *Carrara*
marble. Anyone expecting

cash tonight wouldn't
be glad to see her (Hope, or
Mercy), though we can
all agree that energy

is a resource
of unparalleled
importance, calling us
closer to this narrowing

circle of desire: *Venez,*
tout le monde! Come,
come, she calls. *The whole*
world is welcome. They respond

by opening fire on her
home, disk-shaped
with a thin, soft rind,
the kind of place

that likes flowers. I stayed
awhile longer because anticipation
is an essential part
of this whole trip,
heard the blender

whirling hope: *Espérer,*
a verb. If you can, use it
to feed those who practice.

II

She Slips a Totem Under Her Pillow

When I am weary of existing
as a city human, I imagine
my body as a bear, gathering blackberries,
making a den, sleeping all winter.

I whisper to my dreaming form:
Your animal nature
thrives not on oil or water, not through air,
but on earth, the weight of it, solid.

When I was a girl, some scientist
put me in a class for the gifted. I thought
we were going to get presents. The teacher
assigned a report instead. Such

disappointment! I went home, placed
my finger on the encyclopedia
for bears. Opened it as if it were
a special occasion, copied every word

in my best printing: *Grizzlies belong*
to a species of bears called Ursus
arctos. They are sometimes called silvertips.
Years pass: I am not a bear but a different

teacher on a class trip where we traipse
all the kids a mile in the dark
for a lecture on survival. Mountain climbers
eat butter to stay warm. I would rather

eat fish. On the way back to the flatlands,
we file past a real bear who watches
through unclosed eyes. Only one child notices,
and no one believes because she is the sort

who sees what is wild. I once knew a girl
who fell in love with a bear forever
towering at the wildlife museum.
Instead of fear, the girl, just steady on

her two human legs, would bare her teeth and growl.
Listen: through deep winter sleep, I hear her.

This Is Not a Test

Read the directions carefully: A lady
lifts you out of class, presents
you with chocolate, and lets you out early,
so that now you are on the other
side of the fence, chain link out of focus,
the rest of the school playing recess. Your friends
rush to the divide, ask why you are inside
out of where they are. I can not answer
any questions about those directions. See
yourself rise, the opposite of a flat
stone thrown into a lake. Concentric circles
street, city, state, country, world. Look at the sample
questions that have been done for you: Loss is to beauty
as air is to voice. Strangeness is to vision as eggs are to cake.

It Was All Brass & Percussion

There was something I was meant to learn, something about loving & being loved, about being in the V of the canyon, the climate Mediterranean, not Athens but more remote—L.A., or maybe Perth, Australia—endemic with *I don't understand you*, marsupial with the large foot. We are born before we are viable. Isolated in a fragment, she declines to elaborate, but it was something to do with tapping the chest, cutting the fruit toward you, daring the knife.

*

Love, when I am away from you, run your hand along kangaroo paws, planted rows of velvet mudras. Zero thumb and forefinger until the tips open into tiny green stars. The ribs expand sideways on inhalation. Open torso, full throat.

*

Look up to see a train in the trees. While you were sleeping, they laid track where nothing was. There are river stones not by the river, flecked with feldspar & mica. Granite cliffs rounded to soft. I am homesick although I have not left the house.

*

Cells act as magnets, each one inducing its own field, rotating clockwise. Observe in the microscope the year of strange convergences: Venus transit, Mercury backward, ring of fire. A woman slipped beach rocks into her pocket & they burned holes straight through the fabric. A great white leaps out of ocean water, lands in the middle of your small boat. *Row, row, row your shore gently back to me.*

*

When he was my father, he held me high on his shoulders, sang out Rex the Lion, as if he were royal, not the ragman. I will forever be your itinerant civil servant. On your watch: liminal time in 24 seconds flat. Between valve & wrist, a pulse.

*

I was trying to do no harm, trying not to hurt. The skin filters. Listen: a boy swallowed liquid peppers, repeats *ouch, ouch, ouch* for hours. A line of children marches through the academy of ancient music. They are headed for the arts & crafts of the wild. They carry large instrument cases, black, as if they were doctors' bags. Their voices trombone over the campus: *I'm gonna be all right, I'm gonna be all right.*

*

Imagine chalk, imagine a circle. Draw it yellow & out of that, one portion. Label it KK for all the things you know you know: keys, locks, cages. Draw a second line, extending perimeter to center. Call it KDK: flying a plane, driving a submarine. What's left: all the rest you didn't know you didn't know—the DKDK portion. For instance: a sousaphone is a marching-band tuba. For instance: if you drummed my sternum inside out, there you'd be, all the knitting ripped apart, gold thread spilling to the floor.

A Retrospective of Birds

Crepuscular
2008
Salt-fixed photogenic drawing negative
The action of light upon sensitive paper

No phone ringing, no calendar page turning. Leaves on the kitchen plants falling. Quiet cooing, mostly silent except for the early morning scratching of sparrows in dirt. Owls are farsighted and unable to see anything clearly within a few centimeters of their eyes. Daylight assumes the tinge of dusk.

Many have attributed the indeterminate time of the piece to ticking of a vintage watch hidden behind the front left corner. If the viewer desires, she may affix headphones and listen to her life tick by: days, weeks, years.

Fledgling
2007
Thin black Sharpie on construction paper
9 x 18

A mourning dove descends over & over on a blue couch, waiting for her mate to emerge from ancient fog. In the far wing, unseen by the viewer, a Hasidic doctor who was once a New York City cab driver applies practical faith. Toward the edge of winter, angels at the reception desk remark on the hidden radiance of the female. With the fierceness of a woman expecting a child, one announces: *Behold how a steady breath earns its plaintive song.*

Time Share

We bought 13 weeks on emotion. Party of the first part,
any illusion we once had of privacy is purely sentimental. One of us
wears a hide of pink sympathetic & a blinking light pinned over her chest.

I have to go with the grave robbers. At least they're industrious. Which is to say
robber barons. Who laid iron ribbons, railroaded minutes
into schedules? Even now
there are those of us who lie willingly
on the tracks, claim rejuvenation by electric current. We are a people
who test birds in wind tunnels, observe & measure the bodies of creatures
who make songs without language.

We're a look-ahead agency.

We slide our tongues across the back of
fortunes, stick them to our foreheads,
bow over the evening & pray
all our misplaced eucalyptus don't collapse. Observe how
a drop in temperature opens a pit in glass, hairlines across
the windshield. Even now
there is something trying to be annealed, two humans paired

under a single umbrella, silver crafted from seedpod, butterfly
leaves hinging open, the quantum leap that takes forever.

And the Hours, They Felt Like Years & the Years, Minutes

[00:00]   One

[01:00]   day, we meet on a ride called Zero Gravity, & it
makes no difference because scientists say time is a
function of memory, not watch. Even when

[02:00]   we fall from the top, fling ourselves

[03:00]   from a suspended catch air device (otherwise known as
SCAD), the perceptual chronometer still blinks

[04:00]   numbers too fast. The ground careens

[05:00]   forward. Lately, our timing has been

[06:00]   off. Last week we met

[07:00]   at the farmers' market, but it would have hardly
registered if not for the cashier who asked who was

[08:00]   first. You said I was but, really, you were already there,
waiting to buy daikon radish, baby bok choi, basil, well
before I arrived. Still mistaken, the woman

[09:00]   asked if we needed change, before catching

[10:00]   our separate gazes, my Chinese broccoli, a gathering
of spring onions with green tails. *You're not together*

[11:00]   she noted, not unkindly, & you responded
Not yet, causing us to turn, face each other

[12:00]   & laugh as she added you up. You placed your things
            in a string bag, before leaving said,

[13:00]   *See you next life.* The watchmaker's children,

[14:00]   well, you can imagine, have shoes, but never know
            what time it is, are caught in analogue, don't speak
            digital, are forever dialing the wrong number

[15:00]   of the sun. He wears four watches around his wrist,
            inconceivably thin. The daughter, she sets her clock

[16:00]   twelve minutes fast & yet is always passing the right
            stop, as if she inhabited the wrong stop-action film. In

[17:00]   the time we shared before, were you the cadaver

[18:00]   on my table, your gallbladder no longer Robin's egg
            blue, but a stunning green olive? How we know this

[19:00]   before death, I have no idea. If that was you, I would

[20:00]   slip off second, year, minute, hour. Lean in close,
            whisper what it is like

[21:00]   to hold your bare heart

[22:00]   in my still ticking hands

[23:00]

[24:00]

The Heart When Separated from the Body

goes on beating
        planted in the body of another
                after emerging undisturbed & temporarily nestled
        in a chest of ice, the same material

        circling the rings of Saturn. It's been
millennia since violence smashed gravity against planet, stripping
                a moon's icy mantle, & a mother once wrote:
        The comets
        Have such a space to cross,

        Such coldness, forgetfulness. Old galaxies
excite scientists. Though research
                has not been confirmed, astronomers
        have glimpsed a smudge of light from nearly 13.2 billion years
        ago: *We're getting close*

        to the era of galaxy birth. Our data
suggests the female swam constantly for nine days without any rest
                and lost her cub while the rest of us were locked
        in litigation with Washington bickering
        about the difference

between threatened and endangered.
You can ask, but I'm pretty sure Pluto is no longer
                              a planet & classified instead as part of
            something more grand,
      a belt of space objects extending

                        beyond Neptune. Somewhere in Russia,
      a circus train broke down in frozen weather, and the pull of cold
                              thrust the bears into hibernation,
which the trainers fought with cups of strong tea and chocolate. *We kept
            them awake but they were too tired*

to perform any tricks. Sometimes I imagine
            all the scientists, photographers, environmentalists,
                              tourists gathered on the tundra,
      waiting for the ice to freeze, so they can hunt seals, only they spar
instead of thrive. It's because of the early thaw, the eating season

            declining, not enough fat. I once read of a man
                  who believed in the resurrection
because having children makes one a coward. Ask any six-year-old,
                  and she will tell you: The heart is the pump of your body,
      a muscle the size of your fist. I once read of a boy

whose heart was so enlarged,
it could be seen beating through his T-shirt, *as if to escape*
its cage of ribs. I sometimes wonder
what happened to those Russian circus
bears, their broken-

down caravan, that carpool of parents lined
up at the gate, all waiting to untether their young into the polar sky—
all except the one whose heart kept
beating past. That mother presses her ear against the wide
expanse,

hears her child's heart
beat inside another child's chest. She kneels down, whispers, *An ellipse*
is when you sit on a circle. It's how planets
orbit the sun.

My Mother Is a Poem

When I call her,

split ragged on the phone, she hears the

blackness, tells me I'll find love again.

You're not exactly an ugly old maid,

she says, and even if you were, there's

someone for everyone. You should see

who some people are with.

My mother says she could never write a

poem. I'd kill myself first, she says,

perfectly serious, and I don't tell her

plenty of poets have. My mother speaks

in metaphor, her words slightly askew.

When my computer crashes, she tells me

to call the geek, as if he lived next

door and were available and might

come over for coffee if I added a little

sugar to the deal.

My mother consults her digital tablet as
if it were an oracle, brings it close to
her mouth, finds out where the nearest
Dress for Less is; marvels at the
slightest applications. She downloaded
Miss Parloa's New Cook Book, all
these recipes from 1882, stewed lamb
tongue and parsnip fried in molasses. I
got such a kick in the ass out of it, she
says, I was up all night reading.

My mother writes for me when we are
driving, so I don't crash the car. She
asks how my poetry is, and I tell her fine
and can she write down that last
line she just said: *I'm so glad I'm living
in this age* she writes on a scrap of
paper I find later, her cursive familiar as
air.

My Cousin, Willie Nelson,

does not know we are related,
but my mother met a woman
who was invited by Willie's
wife to Thanksgiving dinner,
*Sat right across from him and
he didn't say a word*

the entire time. My mother,
ever loyal, says maybe Willie
didn't want guests, maybe he
just wanted to be left alone.
She tells me about an ancestor
of hers, Willie's and mine,
who used to read the

Jewish newspaper, right to
left: I thought he was reading
the *Forward* backward, isn't
that the craziest thing? There
are photos of Willie on my
mother's bedside table, all red

bandana, cracked lines, and
bearded face. I can see where
my mother would want to
keep close to such a man,
though two husbands dead,
she knows well enough how
that story

ends. I can't believe how God
let me get away with all the
stuff I got away with and I'm
still alive, she says, sounding
like Willie when he sings like
cousin Patsy, all of

us kin and crazy, on the road
again, blue eyes crying in the
rain.

My Brother Visits Our Mutual Place of Birth

and we go to the farmers' market, not
where our mother worked back in the '60s
for Gilmore Bank, but the one on Tuesday
afternoons, walking distance to our house,
one-eighth the size of his. I pop a free

blackberry into my mouth, and when
he says he's never tasted a blackberry,
I don't ask, How is it you still eat
baloney and iceberg lettuce? Instead, we
stop so he can taste: *All the seeds!* he

says. He has driven north from eucalyptus
and lemon groves to visit his cloistered
urban sister. Yesterday, we ventured
to the Natural History Museum
in search of dinosaur bones. I touched one,

sixty-five million years old. It was Free
Day, and every child in L.A. was with us,
wearing a little backpack and pressing
in to see savannah elephants, of which
only six-hundred thousand remain

in the wild. We drove for miles in cross-town
traffic to snare a corned beef sandwich because
there are no delis where my brother lives,
though there are Jewish people. They wander
the San Diegan diaspora hunting

for a good danish, which my brother did
not find here: this one was both dry and slightly
undercooked. On the freeway, my brother drives
every car he owned as a teenager: the pale
yellow Camaro with the black roof; the Firebird;

the Mazda truck with the Hawaiian-print
curtains sewn by one and not the other
of his girlfriends. My brother remembers
the spray booth he made out of our childhood
garage; the Bondo bodywork, the spring break

sanding of the second girlfriend: *Now that
was love!* He's cruising Van Nuys Boulevard;
he's racing Candy Apple Red, still young
and not yet knowing
the danger of an engine more powerful than its body.

Stop, As in Two-Way

I.

An old Datsun 210, square as
a kid might draw a car, stops
at the corner, a real stop, not
a California pause, but the kind
of stop where you need to shift
back into first gear. A woman
crouches on the sidewalk, bike still
behind her, sideways on the grass.
She is wearing sunglasses and
kneeling like praying, one hand
stretched out, luring a lizard onto
a house of cards.

2.

In the parking lot of Bob's
Market, right outside the door,
the most noble mare, quiet
until a mother lifts her
daughter into the saddle,
inserts a quarter, and both
gallop into the sunset, not
white molded fiberglass,
but sheltering wild.

Prickly Pear Cactus with Deciduous & Evergreen

No fruit yet, only wide paddles of
sharp flat, each plane connected
as in a child's drawing, loop-de-loop
and piled high, one atop another. From this distance
the spikes, barely visible. Only the sun
shows them standing, like hair on an arm when
fingertips touch Styrofoam, like fine needles

      charged with light. Why is it: rings remain

circled inside trunk? There once was a house
where a small girl played Chopin, her feet hovering
above the clean oak floor. Who planted the purple
outside her red door? Tell me: can you see
the bud in the green, rock in the hammer, arrow in the blue
cypress tree?

Tired of all who come with words but no language,

a man shipwrecks an ocean &

we recognize each other, broken-

hearted. *I did not fly*

into space to make history, says a third

crash-landed, emerging from her little capsule,

silk-strung waves behind her. They fished

out all our earthly bodies, emptied

their contents to find notes filled with

accidentals. I should know, I composed

them. The first said: *Last visit,*

the general consensus was

that we were happy. Back when

we were alive, the man hosted

a show called *24 Hours.* Now

cancelled, I asked how was it possible

to capture all those images

over a single day? He confessed

it took much longer & I forgave the slippage

of time. *Even now I love you,*

despite your misplaced optimism &—

something else—I couldn't quite decipher

my own hand, strangely wrinkled after

all this time under water. The ink

of the last missive bleached out altogether,

no words, only two folds creasing

worn fiber, silent & filled with sweet

nothings, a flag you'd salute anywhere.

Urgent Care

It's not the same place as the Be Well Clinic. There are angels on the ceiling, gilded. One human stands facing another. They are not quite the same height, but their foreheads are touching. *You are so dear to me, how did that happen?* He gave me an encyclopedia of knowing, A-E. *Darling, I would give you every volume.* There was that Reverend America guy, preaching the word off a little room, an annex of textiles, thick woven yarn. The hair of my friend is falling out, masses of blond curls, exposing a dark patch on bare scalp. Her mother says, I haven't seen that beauty mark since before you were born. Graffitied letters on the outer wall: *Soy tu rey y tu mi reina*: I am your king & you are my queen. Drink me. Slow heat scans the body, baffled. I hope you diagnose something beautiful with cello, something with strings & shaking, *tremulo*. Noted on the medical chart: not my grandmother's nerve-dead hands, but some other loop, glass flutes in a sycamore shell, open, white, prehistoric.

My To-Do's

- do not include brain surgery,
- pop of rain,
- hiss of match striking
- a grainy page—
- 29 lines of turquoise,
- thin margin of magenta. No,
- my list wants to know
- will you
- rescue her exiled soul,
- travel to Macedonia,
- whirl her palpable human
- on your apricot kitchen floor? There
- was once a pair
- of eagles, injured &
- separated & when they were
- brought together, it was as if
- they had never failed
- the wild. The female is
- fierce, refuses to check off
- any possibility
- that doesn't
- insist: Love,
- always fly
- by my side. Love,
- kindly arrive
- soon. Love, will you
- make me a bride
- again? Answers always:
- I do.

The Heart of Screenland

It's essentially a dramedy, by which
I gathered he was in the industry of making

the unreal true. Somebody
with a dog named Lucky gave me

a plastic bag of beans from his garden. I planted
them deep in my belly, and out grew

the most exquisite stalk, taller than the hill
I see when I look up.
                                        My neighbor on the corner
is dying, more quickly than most. Yesterday

I passed this note pinned to the trunk of a
tree I pass every day:

                    Thank you for your honesty
and compassion towards me. May God bless you. I would like to

see you some day.

The Loss of Incandescent Light

If I could find a class called tenderness, I'd enroll tomorrow. I know

it looks like I'm speaking English, but I'm not. There was some talk

of spangle, some soul confusion, a *glissade* of rain on outstretched

tongue. I knew a woman, she stored her burned-out bulbs

in their original box, so that you could never tell

if you were running low, or simply needed to plant

what you already had. It took months to assemble

her intricate sparkle of heat & glow. It was as if

you were being inducted into some secret something, placing

flag on planet, dazzled & unfurling. Accordingly, she wired

a rocket scientist. His middle name was Venus,

no kidding. He told me Edison had purchased his birthplace,

but on his last visit was shocked to find it still lit

by candles & lamps. I used to do search & rescue,

so I know what we're up against. I wondered if I could

become a comet. *That frozen flying night sky, pardon my*

shining taxi, pardon my golden wing. Evenings, she places filaments

under switchplates. Assures me this current isn't so much radical

as evolutionary. Keeps falling from another drowsy

thought, rouses another crackled thing.

Lines Composed Inside the Rings of the Bodhi Tree

Everything before
this has been a
prelude, every
breath a practice

for death: As demand
became more frivolous,
metal types became
less tensile, and karma

bound men and women
in an endless cycle
of rebirth into painful
lives. Perhaps if

they moved away
from this place where
all their children
had died, their luck

would be different. One day
they took off the blinders,
set down the pack, moved
both hands in an arc,

to indicate a flow
of tears. The Italians
were so touched, they sent
a collection of bells,

and all the women
of the village—and from

far beyond—came to see,
creeping in and out
in a hushed silence
and serving as guidance

to craftsmen engaged
upon royal work.

Ladder of Angels Descends North of LAX

First there was the lopping off the top, the trucks, the human rearranging of earth, but
       Before that, there was the rising up of erosion and faults. Now there are steps
Some of us climb. Some take the path, feet pressing into dust, past the eye of the needlegrass,
       Sweet licorice, feathered wild. Poppy circles, sea lavender bleached to white.
Along the way up, a wet trail of memory, striped spiral of snail toward the center, the city
       Receding, turn to see the Wilshire Corridor from the last Century Towers to the
Federal Building, stretched out like a bowling alley in some summer blockbuster movie,
       Godzilla stepping west to the ocean away from the Hollywood sign nestled in its
Hill, away from the studios where they film versions of real life, click the heels of your
       Ruby slippers and repeat: *There's no place like home.* We wind the path or walk
The steps like Russian nomads, rising up, rising down, the traffic on the street like waves
       Approaching and breaking into a woman's voice on a cell, a man striking a
Gamelan, filling hollow notes with sound. Someone says our bodies reflect our listening,
       And I wonder who else hears our souls whispering as they hover six inches over
Our heads. The body will not always be beautiful, but it will always be blessed. Slow
       Drops fall on the observation deck encircled by ocean that used to be clouds, our
Collective breath filling the basin of where ancient fish used to swim. You can see their
       Vertebrae sometimes in the thin lines of cirrus sky or when the ground firms after
Rain, the steep rise of spine curving us to a choice of road or overlook, and what kind of
       Choice is that? Halfway between urban and heaven, inner gardens sandblasted
Golden, a woman who has been crying looks up at the exact moment someone else feels
       Breath animate the body, looks up to see her face, all our radiant faces, holy,
Holy, holy.

Birds of Paradise

Because you will not remember this day,

as if torn from my notebook and tossed

into the elevator that climbs you silently through

the roof of the building, listen to ceiling opening

to sky, a blue such as you've never tasted,

soft around the throat, a flock of swallows

winging out. Anyone could see it was always West

we'd settle home. Somewhere more Chevy to the levee

than lonely street of desire, somewhere green

palms rustle snow. We'd join a triangle of birds, the far

left tip. Mourning dove flutters herself years down

the track, a promise of orange blossom breathed into lavender

lungs. The fact is we are all in it for the trees, *je t'aime, mon petit*

choux, je t'aime. When the beak opens, place these words gently in the mouth

and sing.

Studying Abroad in the Country of Love

My French teacher was dying the year I studied *je m'appelle* in the mirror, a distant relation, charming, sophisticated. Courage comes from *le cœur*, the heart, leading out from the center. Years later: *Madamoiselle*, how many languages do you know? *Mes étudiants*, that would be one.

*

She was in love with a translator, yearned to give syntax over. A poet who worked at Microsoft warned her not to betray her original tongue. Be passionate about writing code, he said. Between mystery and love, you want to triangulate the language.

*

She walked into an equation scrawled on the white board: $A \neq B$, which she took to mean: metaphors should be flipped like coins, tossed into a fountain or placed on the sockets of eyes.

*

She thought she had given him the boot, but when she reached over and lifted the latch, he was in the trunk, knocking to get out.

*

He was working on his own legends. Where are my angels, my explosions? Where are my dancing animals, elephants charging on darkened savannahs?

*

They met at the intersection of high plain & sky. I keep trying to connect, she said, it's the hardest thing.

*

"Terminal Étude" is the title of a poem translated by Alissa Valles. It refers to one of the terminals at Fryderyk Chopin Airport in Warsaw, where Valles had to wait several hours for a delayed flight. It could also mean *the last study* or even *study for the end*: we two who were one.

*

She once saw a man with π tattooed over his heart. Did that mean it went on forever? Should she have stopped him, asked him if it hurt?

*

When I was a girl, I had a crush on Lincoln, all sad eyes and stooped shoulders. I thought I could heal him, heal the whole country of sad.

*

I will find you, ready or not. Are you hiding behind the rock? Tucked inside in the tree's spire? Are you drifting down the aisle, bride to the nave of the green heart?

*

The Hmong toss balls at one another to find a mate, but it's not a game. If you court love in the New Year, it's a serious endeavor. You are approaching a beautiful girl, probably with her mother behind her. It's intimidating, like approaching love should be.

*

Who's your favorite Beatle? he asked, hoping for a resemblance. *Quelle question!* How can you not love a man who promises the sun, calls you little darlin', breaks into laughter at the end of the song?

*

He showed her how to download the application for new languages. She tilted her ear a little to the left, learned the words for chandelier, cut glass, bow against gut, moving his fingers along the fret of her instrument.

*

At the end of those French movies, it always says *Fin*, which I take to mean: it is finished, but it is not the end.

A Retrospective of Birds

Unmooring

2009

Ritual vessel filled with human clothing, dislocation, open spaces

A seagull separated from the colony fixes her glass eye on a kayak navigating a small strait to the sea. A strip of turquoise, dark blue with orange bisecting, completes the backdrop of the sky. Below, the water, endlessly rocking. No poetry can soothe a bird's desire for freedom.

The kayak itself is constructed of hardwood, softened in freshwater and bent to assume a shapely form. Some say its body recalls that of a woman, the stepping in, the settling, the patient oar placed into and through.

Migration

2010

Illuminated manuscript, vast

An owl in its high pine, disguised
by the glare of street lamps,

keeps watch, wings
silent. A woman walks

next to the darkened grass,
her body a cache

of emeralds, hidden startling
presence. A ship stores treasure

in its hull, making its long
way across the sea.

Four Essays About My Father

I.

Why he hanged himself?   First off,

there was not enough

beauty:

Who could be

happy driving a Gremlin—

orange, not sweet mandarin,

but vegetative, nonaerodynamic—

back & forth to work   a civil servant job he hated

and did not pay

nearly as much as Mr. Fine

across the street,

who still wasn't home   long after   my father

ate dinner with his children,

walked his little one   around the block, lifted her up

on the mailbox,   explained how

crickets   sang,

rubbing their long legs together

like violins.

2.

My father kept

    no photograph   I ever saw

of his brother   who shot himself   or of

    his sister   who was his favorite, dead too soon

        of leukemia. Didn't speak

of them, only said, Live

    fast, die young, and make a good-

      looking corpse: strange advice

to give his daughter,   a little girl   with a curl

    right in the middle   of her forehead,   picture always

  in his wallet,   close to his chest

      pocket, opposite my brother's smile,

and our mother   in a borrowed

      dress,   seed pearls

  all over.

My brother,

        who is our father's physical

double, says Dad was ill—

        something with his eyes,   couldn't stand

the thought of

        going blind,   maybe had the same

window defect

        as in my retina,   black spot in light

created by slow leakage. In any case

        it wasn't his heart: that was

                still beating

        after they cut him down.   I know this because

my brother,

        of-age young,   next-of-heart kin   proved heart enough

to pull

        the plug.

4.

He let me climb

                onto his island   stretched out

on the den chair, reclining, open;

                      endured questions

about moles,   age spots,   imperfections,

              never said   the old man

was raining, pouring,   broken:

    only waited

            until I was too big to fit

pressed chest to chest,   rising & falling,

            palm calming my breath. How

many times I fell asleep

            like that, he never folded   in the chair until I

woke up again.

When Not in Rome,

I awake early without
you who are
in a room all
apricot & cherry. In
Portuguese it's very,
very poetic.

All those little bottles
carrying wisps of messages—

Don't let me
translate these things:
the sailor, the harbor,
the shore. Go on,

take the boat. Take
the salt, take the whole
curved ocean. You know
you can't live
what you were
living before.

The Mapmaker Is Revealed to Be a Woman

We were navigating the sad, pulling branches off trees with chainsaws

      & bulldozing trunks. Startled birds

did not know where to go in the chaos.

         Would you be able to survive in the wilderness, have the capacity

     to banish what haunts? She had a way of

moving across a page. To describe

     her as a puzzle maker wouldn't do it justice. Everyone thought

she was a great constructor, her diagrams wide open, but she was

       discontented. *I've been so general*, she complained. *I long for*

detail & am ashamed of my ambition. And if she had you

     on her knee, it was fascinating the way she seemed to

draw whole constellations out of voice & air. She conjured up a cake once,

       poppy seed lemon, its circular shape

     spiraling the sun. Somewhere in a northern port city, children

devoured mangoes inside the hull of a ship, & those of us

       still on earth pointed from our huts

     to her floating wicker basket & thought

surely she would fall out of the sky.

The Daughter Who Flew Through the Atmosphere & Into a State of Nature

If she were in Ovid, she might be

a tree, not Daphne, but another

racing   through a blue slit

in the sky. Up, up—

the houses, miniature

squares. The streets,

nowhere she need ever travel

again. Some tangles

turn to knots, their laces

undone. Here,

sweet mortal, feel

the stepping out of shoe

into limb, the rising, root,

               the leafing.

Spring & All That

time, you have been tucked in my bag for weeks, a small blue
version of you, I carry all spring on my shoulder—farmers'

market, bookstore, doctor's office, where I am kept
waiting an inordinately long while, only I hardly notice

that I am perched on the thinnest of tissues
because for the first three hours, I have closed

my eyes to florescent buzz, acoustic ceiling tiles dotted
with pinholes, let my consciousness enlarge

on the examining table—not so much imaginative
act as practical surrender of a woman who has waited

weeks for this appointment & now finds herself
open gown to the front, almost attended & why not

give up the illusion anything else matters? Nothing
so much as stainless steel, glass containers, Sharps

collector of needles, instruments to examine
eyes, ears, & scale. Oh, lifetime certified jewel movement,

measure my blood in calibrated increments as it circulates
through the chambers of my heart, in which the EKG detects

slight variations, & my doctor, when she finally appears,
says *Enter a new world, and have there freedom*

of movement. Days later, I run past a woman wearing a T-shirt
that says *breaking hearts, fixing bones* & I kid you not,

past a red wheelbarrow

my neighbor has wheeled to the corner,
not glazed because it has not rained in weeks but lettered white

on the side: *True Temper USA,* & I can feel my heart too much
inside my chest wanting the glaze of your pulse, wanting

poetry not prose, wanting some good doctor to press the beauty
of my irregular heartbeat to his mouth, never let me go.

By Accident

As if some quick Eurydice

                    set down both wings

        when she witnessed

geese fly into fire,

      first one engine, then the other

burn

      into exhausted smoke. It wasn't

                bullet or bomb or other

human error,

        only birds flying in their way—

                effortless, soaring, without guile or training.

    Our vessel glided

        on the water

           as better-fated birds skim a surface, silent

      without splash,

                steel-bellied feathers unruffled. They say

she walked the empty aisles twice,

          searching the upside down sky

    for us, passengers lined up

          on the chill river,

                boats speeding from shore

to return us to the living.

Note to (Future) Self:

That burden you set down
not so long ago—it was found
on a luggage carousel in Rome,
merry-go-rounding to cheers
in the Colosseum, where you fought
your last battle, that brilliant move
right before the final bow,
the night you cut your own heart out—
tender, oozing—and planted it in the back
garden. Check the messages
in your in-box: One says please forgive
the intrusion—they had to spring the lock
because any unclaimed bag is suspect
these days, you know how it is. No clothes
left inside, only a heart of (I know
you'll say cliché) (but think genuinely) 24-karat
gold—must have weighed a fortune, all that
crucibled purity. They're sending it to your new address,
knew it was yours from the dirt-smeared tag.

The Receptivity of Astonishment to Trees

i

black phone with red square
in the corner, who calls you
& will you answer
or will someone
press an oval button—
redial, hold, conference,
transfer?

ii

hello, checkerboard floor,
gray, white, gray
under years of feet &

iii

oh, door of clear
fir, rings still visible,
hinged elbow, stainless
handle that turns

iv

outside a line
of young ginkgos,
as in those films
where the hero twirls,
skims up walls
with no wires—

v

mountains cradle

vi

arrows of pine silhouetted,
& off the white-lined side
of the road, someone has
adorned
your branches with dazzled
globes.

After Death Comes & Has Your Eyes,

verdurous laughter will
sprint down the weeks
of late April, box her
two ears, first left, then

right, until spring's cheeky
accomplice taps messages
in Morse code—quick, slow, the
quickening begins—accompanies

dots & dashes in their
daily run. Amiable & serene,
the insomniacs venture out
to ravish rhyme under the visual

assurance of one who hears
Cyrano vanquish a serenade,
opens a parasol for the taciturn
in dour need of lighting a green

morning. And tea & cherries
will quell the day with our
supreme concurrence that
life is yes, new,

never has been seen.

—after Cesare Pavese

A Retrospective of Birds

Lost & Found

2011
High-resolution pixilation

This digitized image depicts two birds reported rescued in last year's news:

The first is Lola, an African gray who made her escape right after the summer solstice. Upon being questioned, Lola's human wondered: *What if Lola just needs a vacation?* Gone 24 days, Lola was discovered two miles away, perched on a pot of geraniums. She was recognized by a scar on her talon, where she had once been clipped by a closing door.

Also pictured [in the dome of the main reading room at the Library of Congress] is a Cooper's hawk that mistook shelter for freedom. Prior to the hawk's release into the wild, she was reported to be *taking the occasional circle swoop around the mural of the figure of human understanding.*

While sounding a field of cornflowers, she hears

not weeds but chimes, delicate waves to helix, silent
asters. Wash your tired eyes and vibrate blue

through hammer, anvil, stirrup—into my oval window, acoustical spiral
staircase to fluid chamber—quick, quick

before thieving vision arrives, and we will make a curved space
to lay our bodies down on blue and blue and blue,

as in a house that used to be a steeple. Do you resonate
her bells? Little snail, uncoil liquid shell, sail blue boat

into patient canal and blossom
hollow labyrinth of bone. Stellars hush crickets, won't you

please—be my listening starling?

Reconnaissance

The agapanthus quiet until

        the earth sends mysterious
tentacles, scapes tall as toddlers
    searching for light,

their inflorescence
        open in the dark,
            lighting our way
down the street
    as we walk,
      lighting the walk, as if

we were on parade, jubilant globes
        of blue and white,
          each world floating,

umbel fastened by stalk as
    astronaut tethered to ship. And

by day, the bees, vibrating
        bodies, moving, breathing,
    whisking pollen from anther,

           stamen of the tiniest flower,

feet threaded with gold.

Lines Composed in the Library of Last Century Furniture

There was a slight shift,
a tremble in the Earth,
followed by a quick
change to the singular

in which she declared *Mine*
must be an anti-slavery
life, served over ice with
lemon peel, flowers,

small, white, or greenish,
in a simple or compound
terminal umbel. Where
an opposition

of direction creates
a tension, it becomes
necessary to
envisage a complete

liberation, specters
of darkness put to flight
by a troop of aerial
spirits. It implies

something of an ordeal,
too; a struggle in which
primal pain will be given
and suffered. *Habeas*

corpus: a Latin term
meaning you are ordered
to have the body. And
I had to use the full

strength of my voice—it chirps,
it hops, it jumps, and sings
all through the summer night.

Notes

"Panorama Highway" makes reference to Marilyn Jorgenson Reece, "the first woman to be registered as a civil engineer and the designer of the San Diego-Santa Monica freeway interchange." In his *Los Angeles Times* obituary on Reece, Dennis McLellan quotes urban critic Reyner Banham's *Los Angeles: The Architecture of Four Ecologies*.

The series "A Retrospective of Birds" makes use of information gleaned from a variety of sources, including National Public Radio, Wikipedia, Whitman's *Leaves of Grass*, and a series of *Los Angeles Times* articles, by Kate Linthicum, on a missing parrot.

"Valiant" draws on popular culture from the 1960s and '70s, including the automobile manufactured by Plymouth; the DC Comics fictional character portrayed on television by Julie Newmar, Lee Meriwether, Eartha Kitt, and Yvonne Craig; and the lyrical anthem by Don McLean as it converges with the annual beauty pageant.

The "mystic poet" of "In Surprise, Arizona" is Rumi, and the italicized line is from his poem, "Someone Digging in the Ground," translated by Coleman Barks and anthologized in *The Soul Is Here for Its Own Joy*, edited by Robert Bly.

The "kind of blue" playing in "Domestic Still Life" is that of the incomparable Miles Davis.

The first italicized line in "We Find Ourselves Immersed" is from Antonio Carlos Jobim's "Águas de Março/Waters of March." The poem is for the Roast family.

"The Situation Room Is Gutted Down to Brick & Bare Floor" refers to the intelligence-management center located in the basement of the West Wing of the White House. The poem also alludes to world events that occurred during the early part of 2011: the civil demonstrations and unrest across the Middle East and North Africa frequently referred to as the "Arab Spring"; the earthquake and subsequent tsunami off the coast of Japan in which three reactors in the Fukushima Daiichi Nuclear Power Plant failed; and the U.S. strike on the northern Pakistan compound of Osama bin Laden.

"She Slips a Totem Under Her Pillow" is for Katherine Chavez.

"And the Hours, They Felt Like Years & the Years, Minutes" refers to an experiment in time perception developed by neuroscientist David Eagleman. Special thanks to Peter Vogel for bringing it to my attention.

In "The Heart When Separated From the Body," Sylvia Plath is the "mother [who] once wrote" *the comets / Have such a space to cross, // Such coldness, forgetfulness.* The italicized lines are from "The Night Dances." The poem is for the family of Sally Menke.

The last lines of "My Cousin, Willie Nelson" recall the popular songs written by Nelson and Fred Rose. Patsy Cline also recorded a version of Nelson's "Crazy." Any relation to the singers is purely imagined.

The title, "Tired of all who come with words but no language," is a line by Tomas Tranströmer. Another line draws from American astronaut Sally Ride: "I did not come to NASA to make history."

Kind thanks to Peter Trachtenberg for some of the language in "Urgent Care," and for his always spot-on suggestions.

"My To-Do's" refers to a pair of rescued eagles tended to by wildlife specialist Wendi Pencille and reported by Michele Norris on National Public Radio's *All Things Considered*.

"Lines Composed Inside the Rings of the Bodhi Tree" refers to the defunct Bodhi Tree bookstore in West Hollywood, California.

Thanks to poet and translator William O'Daly for a day at Caltech, where "Studying Abroad in the Country of Love" began its convergence.

"Spring & All That" borrows its title and the line "Enter a new world, and have there freedom of movement" from the 1923 work by William Carlos Williams.

"By Accident" alludes to the emergency landing of US Airways Flight 1549 in the Hudson River on January 15, 2009, after bird strikes caused both jet engines to fail. The aircraft was piloted by Captain Chesley B. Sullenberger and First Officer Jeffrey Skiles.

The staircase pictured on the front cover is located at the Baldwin Hills Scenic Overlook, a California State Park. It is a collaboration of Safdie Rabines Architects and the landscape design firm of Wallace Roberts and Todd.

Acknowledgments & Thanks

Grateful acknowledgment is made to the editors and staffs of the journals in which the following poems first appeared, sometimes in slightly different versions:

Anti—: "It Was All Brass & Percussion"
Atlas Review: "A Retrospective of Birds"
Colorado Review: "Panorama Highway" and "She Slips a Totem Under Her Pillow"
CRATE: "Domestic Still Life"
Construction Magazine: "Birds of Paradise," "My To-Do's," and "O, steepled world,"
FIELD: "And the Hours, They Felt Like Years & the Years, Minutes"
Grist: "Urgent Care"
Hawai'i Pacific Review: "We Find Ourselves Immersed"
Permafrost: "The Heart When Separated From the Body" and "The Moon Over Mars"
Puerto del Sol: "The Daughter Who Flew Through the Atmosphere & Into a State of Nature"
The Offending Adam: "Ladder of Angels Descends North of LAX" and "The Mapmaker Is Revealed to Be a Woman"
Santa Clara Review: "Spring & All That"
Seneca Review: "Studying Abroad in the Country of Love"
Sparkle & Blink: "Liquid Takes the Shape of Its Container," "The Loss of Incandescent Light" and "When Not in Rome,"
Spillway: "My Father, on the Small Screen"
Stone Hobo: "In Surprise, Arizona"
Zócalo Public Square: "My Brother Visits Our Mutual Place of Birth"
ZYZZYVA: "My Cousin, Willie Nelson" and "My Mother Is a Poem"

A gathering of poems in this collection appeared in the chapbook *Valiant* (Finishing Line Press, 2012).

"The Loss of Incandescent Light" was reprinted in *Women in Metaphor,* edited by Maria Elena B. Mahler, with original paintings by Stephen Linsteadt (Natural Healing House Press, 2013).

"Note to (Future) Self" was included in *Beyond the Lyric Moment: Poetry Inspired by Workshops with David St. John,* edited by Jim Natal, Cathie Sandstrom, and Lynne Thompson (Tebot Bach, 2014).

"The Receptivity of Astonishment to Trees" appears as lyrics in an original musical composition by Adam Borecki.

Warm thanks to Alain Borer for his translation into French of "When Not in Rome," which appeared as "Ailleurs qu'à Rome" in a special issue of *Levure littéraire*, edited by Hélène Cardona. And to Alexa Mergen for inviting the English version to reside at *Yoga Stanza*, accompanied by an effervescent half-moon.

Heartful gratitude as well to all who helped to bring this book into the world, especially:

Augsburg College MFA and Howling Bird Press staff, including Cass Dalglish, director; Amanda Symes, Ashley Cardona, and Kevin Matuseski, associate editors; and John Gaterud, publisher.

Beloved teachers: Angie Estes, Mark Irwin, Jim Krusoe, and David St. John.

Valiant champions: Sarah Maclay, Gretchen Mattox, and Lynn Melnick.

Clear-sighted photographer: Peter Figen.

Temple guardians: Tang, Chado, and the little gray cat.

Home team: the Miller, Hennes, Jacobs, and Vogel families. Special thanks to Dr. Jerrold Alan Hennes, Peter Vogel, and Dr. Lillian Brown Vogel for enduring love and support.

Fellow travelers inside and outside the Heart of Screenland: Echo Horizon School; Ashland University; the Napa Valley Writers' Conference; the Idyllwild Arts Foundation; the Ruskin Art Club; Beyond Baroque Literary Arts Center; L'École supérieure des beaux-arts in Tours, France; the Baldwin Hills Scenic Overlook; Spirit Rock Meditation Center; Santa Monica Yoga; and the University of Southern California.

And to the ones who bought me here: my loving fathers, Robert Hennes and William R. Enz; my beautiful, shining mother, Ilene Estelle. Love beyond words.

The Author

Marci Vogel was born and raised in Los Angeles, California. Her poetry, essays, and translations have appeared in *FIELD*, *Poet Lore*, *Plume*, *Jacket2*, and *Drunken Boat*, among others. A first-generation college student, she is currently a doctoral candidate in the Creative Writing and Literature Program at the University of Southern California. *At the Border of Wilshire & Nobody* is her first full-length collection.

Special Thanks

The students, faculty, and staff in the MFA in Creative Writing Program at Augsburg College wish to thank the many supporters of Howling Bird Press who participated in "Give to the Max" in 2014—and, especially, the following individuals and organizations for their generous support for the publication of this book: Gary Johnson, William Dalglish, Louis Branca, Jörg & Angie Pierach, Blueroad Press, and Cass Dalglish.